# Grammar Practice Book

Scott Foresman

**Editorial Offices:** Glenview, Illinois • Parsippany, New Jersey • New York, New York
**Sales Offices:** Reading, Massachusetts • Duluth, Georgia • Glenview, Illinois
Carrollton, Texas • Ontario, California

**Editorial Offices**
Glenview, Illinois • Parsippany, New Jersey • New York, New York

**Sales Offices**
Reading, Massachusetts • Duluth, Georgia • Glenview, Illinois
Carrollton, Texas • Ontario, California

ISBN 0-328-00664-5

18 19 20 21 22 23 DBH 10 09 08 07

# Table of Contents

**Unit 2** Sentences

## *Take a Closer Look*

**Unit 3** **Nouns**

## *Let's Learn Together*

## Unit 4 Verbs

## Unit 5 Adjectives

**Unit 6** **Pronouns and Sentences**

## *Surprise Me!*

Name ______________________________

## Circle.

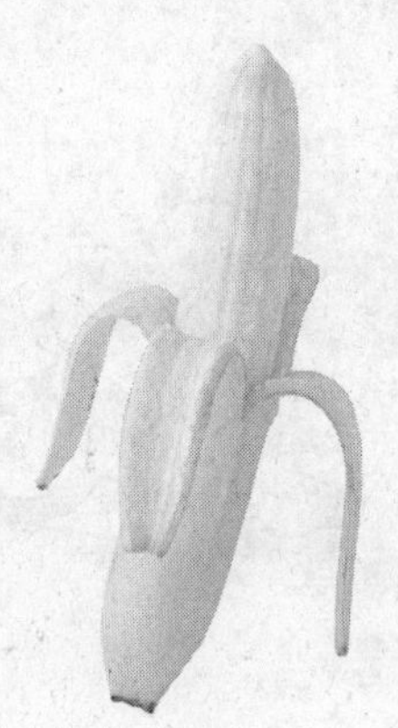

**Directions:** Circle an animal, a person, and a place.

**Home Activity:** Look at pictures and label persons, places, aminals, and things.

Name ________________________________ 

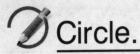

## Circle.

**Directions:** Circle three things you can do.

**Home Activity:** Ask your child to tell about his or her favorite activity.

Name ______________________________

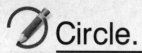

## Circle.

**Directions:** Circle the person in each row.

**Home Activity:** Have your child draw and label a picture of himself or herself playing with friends.

Name ______________________________

## Draw a line.

bats

hats

See a bat and a hat.

## Draw.

I see a big bat and a tall hat.

**Directions:** Draw lines to match the words and pictures. Draw a picture of the sentence.

**Home Activity:** Have your child make up a sentence and draw a picture of it.

Name ______________________

## Circle.

**Directions:** Circle the pictures of places.

**Home Activity:** Help your child label places in pictures.

Name ______________________________

**The children ride bikes.**

A **sentence** is a group of words that tells a complete idea.

**Find** each sentence.
**Draw** a line under each one.

1. Two girls
   books
   Two girls read books.

2. Bob paints a picture.
   Bob
   a picture

3. sings a song
   Ms. Fox
   Ms. Fox sings a song.

**Notes for Home:** Your child identified complete sentences. ***Home Activity:*** Talk about what you did today. Have your child write a complete sentence that describes one thing you did.

Name ______________________________

**Find** the sentence.
**Write** the sentence.

1. Kim found    Kim found a cat.

______________________________

2. She pats her pet.    her pet

______________________________

3. The cat    The cat eats food.

______________________________

4. drinks milk    The cat drinks milk.

______________________________

**Notes for Home:** Your child wrote complete sentences. ***Home Activity:*** Have your child make up two sentences about a favorite game.

Name ______________________________

**RETEACHING**

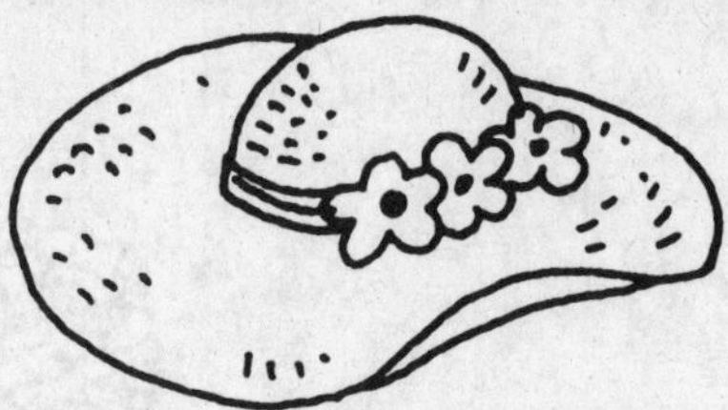

**The hat** is big.

The **naming part** of a sentence
names a person, animal, or thing.
It usually tells who or what does something.

**Draw** lines to match the two parts to make sentences.
**Circle** the naming part.

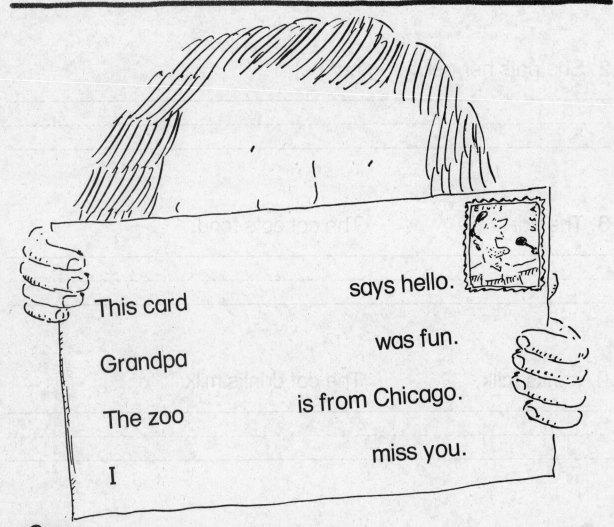

| | |
|---|---|
| This card | says hello. |
| Grandpa | was fun. |
| The zoo | is from Chicago. |
| I | miss you. |

**Notes for Home:** Your child matched sentence parts. ***Home Activity:*** Write subjects (*Our dog, Your hat, My nose*) on cards. Have your child choose a card and use the subject to make up or write a sentence.

Name ______________________________

Complete each sentence.
**Write** the naming part.

Mary Plays

1. ____________________ feeds the fish.

Look at Jon

2. ____________________ waters the plants.

Bill and Tim Run away

3. ______________________________
pass out snacks.

4. What job can you do?

______________________________

______________________________

**Notes for Home:** Your child wrote naming parts of sentences. ***Home Activity:*** Have your child draw a picture of a family member. Then have him or her write a sentence, using that family member's name as the subject of the sentence.

Name ___________________________



RETEACHING

| My father plants a tree. | |
|---|---|
| **Naming Part:** | **Action Part:** |
| My father | plants a tree. |

A sentence has two parts.
The **action part** tells what a person or thing does.

**Underline** the action part.

1. Tom and I plant many seeds.

2. A bird eats some seeds.

3. Other seeds grow into flowers.

4. My father waters the flowers.

**Notes for Home:** Your child identified predicates—parts of sentences that tell action—in sentences. ***Home Activity:*** Say the name of a favorite television show character or story character. Have your child make up a sentence about what that character can do.

Name ______________________

**Finish** each sentence.
**Read** each naming part.
**Write** the correct action part from the box.

| runs fast | fly away | play ball |
|---|---|---|

1. The boys ______________________.

2. Lee ______________________.

3. The birds ______________________.

**Notes for Home:** Your child wrote predicates in sentences. ***Home Activity:*** Visit a favorite place. Have your child describe in complete sentences what people or animals are doing. Then ask him or her to repeat the action parts of their sentences.

Name ______________________________



RETEACHING

**Bike rides a Dad.**

This group of words does not make sense.

The words are not in the correct order.

**Dad rides a bike.**

This group of words makes sense.

The words are in the correct order.

**Draw** a line under the words in the correct order.

1. We ride in the park. Park ride in the we.
2. My flat is tire. My tire is flat.
3. Bike fixes my Dad. Dad fixes my bike.
4. Do you ride a bike? Do bike ride a you?

**Write** each missing word.

5. My fast moves bike.

My ____________ moves ____________.

**Notes for Home:** Your child identified the correct word order in sentences. ***Home Activity:*** Write a sentence with your child. Use scissors to cut between the words, and have your child put the words in the correct order.

Name ______________________

**Write** an X next to the words that are **not** in sentence order. **Write** them in sentence order. Do not write the sentences that are in the correct order already.

1. Pets have many we. ______

2. Rabbits live in our yard. ______

3. Pets feeds the Mom. ______

4. What pet do you want? ______

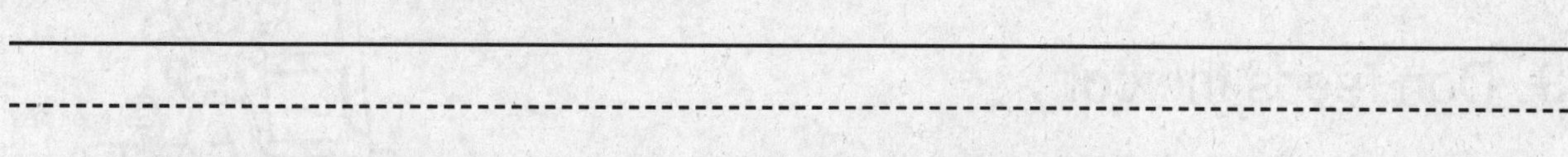

**Notes for Home:** Your child wrote words in the correct order in sentences. ***Home Activity:*** Have your child look at magazine pictures. Say two sentences (one incorrectly) to describe it. Have your child identify the sentence with words in the correct order.

Name ______________________________



RETEACHING

Mom has a paint can.

A **statement** tells something.
Begin a statement with a **capital letter.**
End a statement with a **period.**

**Draw** a line from each statement to the correct picture.

1. Jen moves the chair.

2. Mom paints the door.

3. Don feeds the cat.

4. Dad cleans the floor.

**Notes for Home:** Your child identified statements that matched pictures. ***Home Activity:*** Have your child draw a picture of a friend doing something. Then have him or her write a statement about what the friend is doing.

Name ______________________

**Match** the sentence parts.
**Write** the statements.

| | |
|---|---|
| The dog | gets cut. |
| The wood | is my pet. |
| Today | is red. |
| My hat | it rains. |

1. ______________________

2. ______________________

3. ______________________

4. ______________________

**Notes for Home:** Your child wrote statements correctly. ***Home Activity:*** Have your child make up statements about the weather today.

Name ______________________________

RETEACHING

**Are you my friend?**

A **question** asks something.
It begins with a capital letter.
It ends with a question mark.

**Draw** a line under each question.

1. Can I come?
   You can come.

2. We can play.
   Can we play?

3. The game is fun.
   Is the game fun?

4. May I have one?
   You may have one.

5. Can you stay?
   I can stay.

**Notes for Home:** Your child correctly identified questions. ***Home Activity:*** Write two statements and two questions. Have your child find the questions and answer them.

Name ______________________________

**Look** at the words.
Use them to **write** a question.

1. my book who has

______________________________

2. will snow fall

______________________________

3. my hat where is

______________________________

4. my ball do you see

______________________________

**Notes for Home:** Your child wrote questions. ***Home Activity:*** Write two sentences about animals. Have your child make up questions about the animals.

Name ______________________________

RETEACHING

| Person | Place | Thing |
|---|---|---|
| woman | zoo | tree |

The word **woman** names a person.
The word **zoo** names a place.
The word **tree** names a thing.

A **noun** names a person, place, or thing.

**Circle** the noun for each picture.
**Write** the word.

| Person | Place | Thing |
|---|---|---|
| boy run | park fun | ride bike |
| 1. ________ | 2. ________ | 3. ________ |

**Notes for Home:** Your child identified nouns—words that name people, places, or things. ***Home Activity:*** Have your child use nouns to label four people, places, and things in your home.

Name ______________________



Color **blue** the nouns that name people.
Color **yellow** the nouns that name things.
Color **green** the nouns that name places.

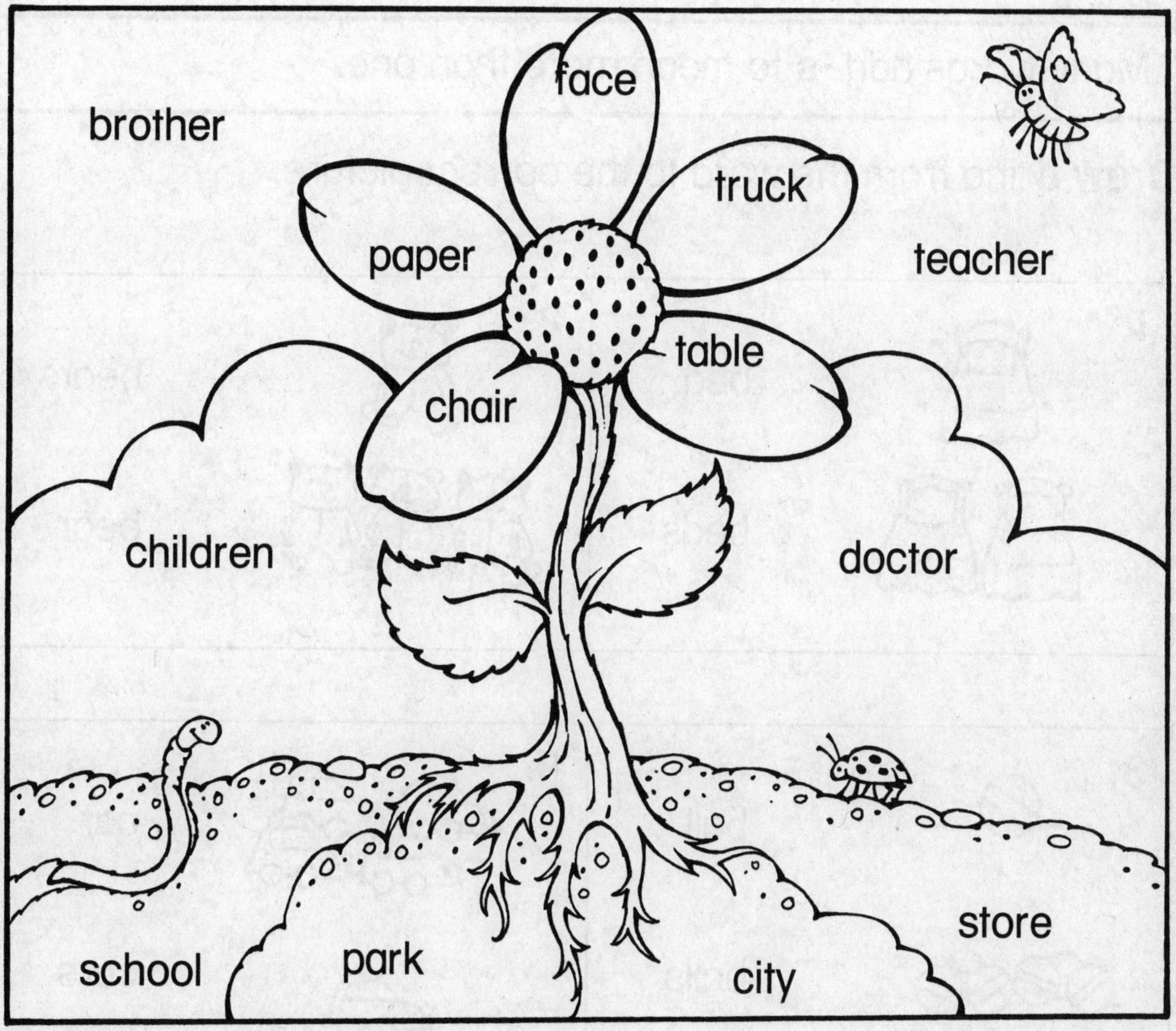

face
brother
truck
paper
teacher
table
chair
children
doctor
store
school
park
city

**Notes for Home:** Your child identified nouns—words that name people, places, or things. ***Home Activity:*** Together, make up a song about people, places, and things you might see in a park.

Name ______________________________

RETEACHING

boy

boys

boy + -s = boys

Many words add **-s** to mean more than one.

**Draw** a line from the word to the correct picture.

| 1. | | 2. | |
|---|---|---|---|
| | bed | | bears |
| | beds | | bear |

| 3. | | 4. | |
|---|---|---|---|
| | ball | | car |
| | balls | | cars |

**Notes for Home:** Your child labeled pictures with singular and plural nouns. ***Home Activity:*** Together, cut out pictures from magazines or newspapers. Have your child use nouns to label the pictures.

Name ______________________

**Trace** the path.
**Follow** the words that mean more than one.

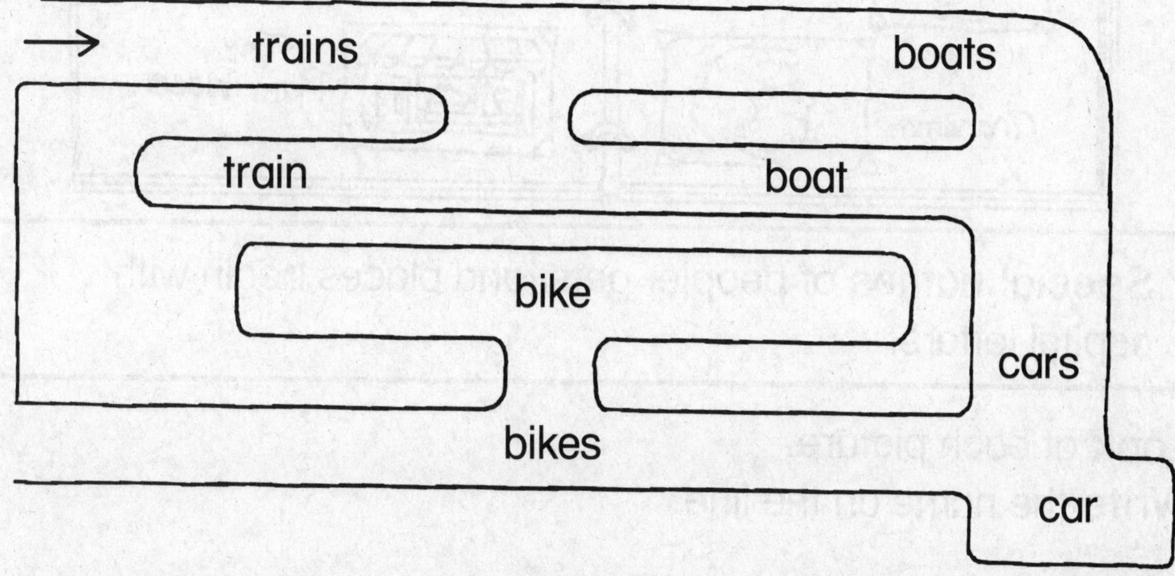


**Write** the correct word on the line.

| worker | workers |
|---|---|

1. The ______________ fixes the road.

| car | cars |
|---|---|

2. Six ______________ are on the street.

**Notes for Home:** Your child identified and wrote plural nouns—nouns that name more than one person, place, or thing. ***Home Activity:*** Ask your child to explain the rule for adding *-s* to nouns that name more than one.

Name ______________________

**Special names** of people, pets, and places begin with capital letters.

**Look** at each picture.
**Write** the name on the line.

Denver  1. I live in ______________________.

Spot  2. My dog is ______________________.

Flo  3. My sister is ______________________.

**Notes for Home:** Your child identified and wrote proper nouns—nouns that name specific people, places, or animals. ***Home Activity:*** Have your child explain the rule for beginning a proper noun with a capital letter

Name ______________________________

**Circle** the special name in each box.
**Write** one special name in each sentence.

| boy | Bob | town | Salem |
|---|---|---|---|
| Fluffy | cat | Aunt Kate | woman |

1. ____________ sits on a chair.

2. ____________ runs around the house.

3. They live in ____________.

**Notes for Home:** Your child identified and wrote proper nouns. ***Home Activity:*** Have your child draw a picture of family members. Have him or her use proper nouns to label the drawing. Make sure your child uses capital letters to write proper nouns.

Name ______________________________

**RETEACHING**

A **title** can come before the name of a person.
A title begins with a capital letter.
It ends with a period.

This is **Mrs. Vargas**.

**Read** the title and the name.
**Write** the title and the name correctly on the line.

1. mrs kay lyons

______________________________

2. dr sal miller

______________________________

3. mr john korn

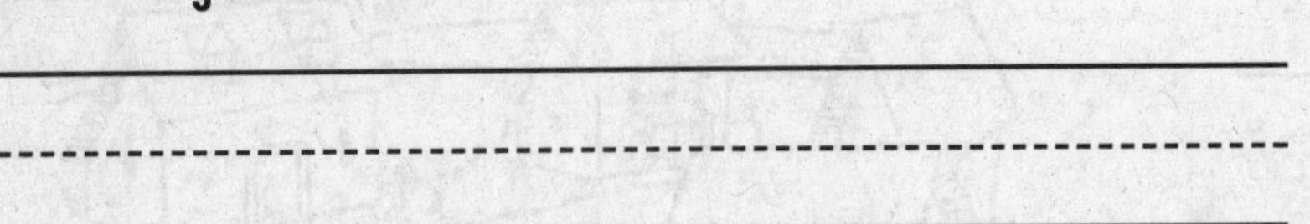

4. mr gil cruz

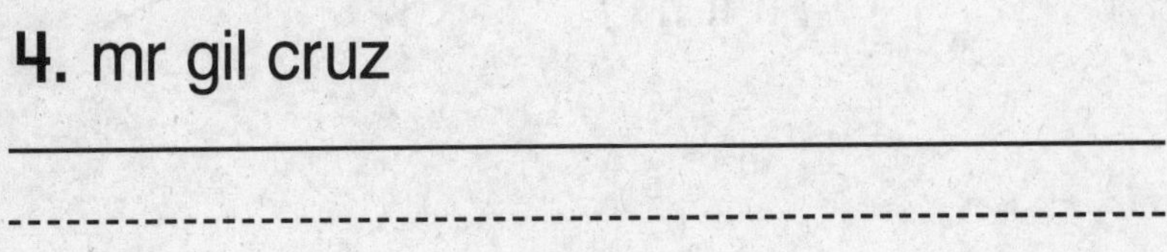

**Notes for Home:** Your child wrote special titles, such as *Dr., Mr.,* and *Mrs.* ***Home Activity:*** Make name tags for family members. Have your child write a title for each person, using correct capitalization and punctuation.

Name ______________________________

**Write** each name correctly.

Monday

dr. billy bear

1. ______________________________

Tuesday

miss wendy wildcat

2. ______________________________

Wednesday

mr. david deer

3. ______________________________

Thursday

mrs. gretchen goat

4. ______________________________

Friday

dr. bobby bee

5. ______________________________

**Notes for Home:** Your child wrote titles, such as *Dr., Mr.,* and *Mrs.,* correctly. ***Home Activity:*** Together, write a story about funny characters with titles (*Dr. Fishface, Mrs. Peanutbutter*).

Name ______________________

RETEACHING

The **boy** saw a **frog**.

A **noun** names a person, place, animal, or thing.
It can be in more than one place in a sentence.

**Circle** the noun in each sentence.
**Write** a noun from the box on the line.

| store | cat | bus | boy |
|---|---|---|---|

1. The ______________ is on the mat.

2. Children ride in a ______________.

3. My dad works in a ______________.

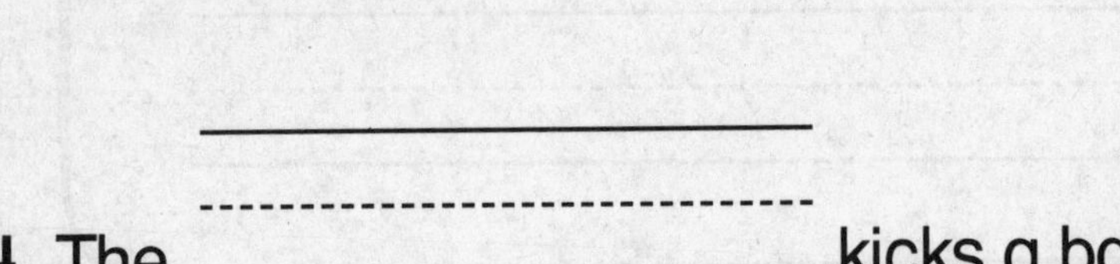

4. The ______________ kicks a ball.

**Notes for Home:** Your child wrote nouns in sentences. ***Home Activity:*** Have your child draw a picture of people or animals doing something. He or she should use two nouns to write a sentence about the picture.

Name ______________________________

**Read** each sentence.
**Circle** the nouns.
**Write** them on the lines.

In spring I run in the rain.

1. ______________ ______________

The rain wets my face.

2. ______________ ______________

In summer I swim in the lake.

3. ______________ ______________

In fall I rake the leaves.

4. ______________ ______________

The leaves are loud under my feet.

5. ______________ ______________

In winter I slide on the snow.

6. ______________ ______________

**Notes for Home:** Your child identified nouns in subjects and predicates of sentences. ***Home Activity:*** Together, write a poem about the seasons. Have your child supply the nouns.

Name ______________________________



| | | | |
|---|---|---|---|
| **Sunday** | **Monday** | **Tuesday** | **Wednesday** |
| **Thursday** | **Friday** | **Saturday** | |

**January**

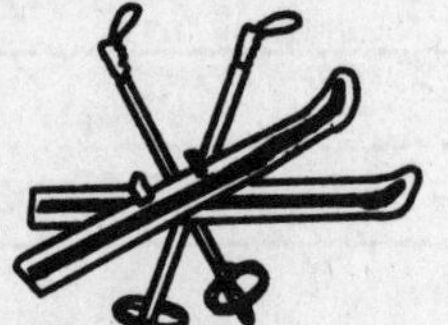
**February**

**March**

**April**

**May**

**June**

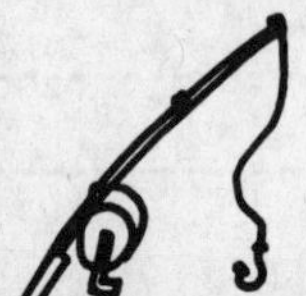
**July**

**August**

**September**

**October**

**November**

**December**

**Days of the week** begin with capital letters.
**Months of the year** begin with with capital letters.

**Write** the correct month.

1. People can fly kites in ______________________.

2. People can swim in ______________________.

**Circle** the name of each day that is written correctly.

3. Sunday monday tuesday Wednesday thursday Friday Saturday

**Notes for Home:** Your child wrote names of months and identified names of days that were written correctly. ***Home Activity:*** Together, create a calendar of family activities. Have your child write the names of the days and months, using capital letters.

Name ______________________________

**Circle** each month that is written correctly.

I. January February March april

may June july

**Read** the days of the week below.
**Write** one to complete each sentence.

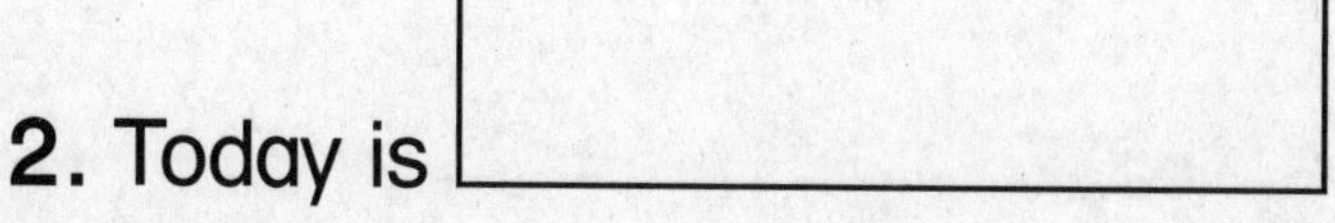

**2.** Today is ______________.

**3.** The next day is ______________.

**4.** We do not go to school on ______________.

| Sunday | Monday | Tuesday | Wednesday |
|---|---|---|---|
| Thursday | Friday | Saturday | |

**Notes for Home:** Your child identified names of months that were written correctly and used names of days in sentences. ***Home Activity:*** Have your child draw a picture of what he or she did today. Then have him or her label the picture with the day, date, and year.

Name ____________________

eat

read

A **verb** is a word that shows action.

**Read** each sentence.
**Draw** a line under each verb.

1. The children run.
2. They sit in the sun.
3. The dogs bark.
4. The birds fly in the sky.
5. Everyone plays in the park.
6. They eat lunch.

**Write** a verb in the sentence.

7. The cats ____________________.

**Notes for Home:** Your child identified verbs—words that name actions—in sentences. ***Home Activity:*** Help your child create a two-box comic strip. Have him or her use verbs to label the action in the comic strip.

Name ______________________________

**Write** the correct verb from the box under each picture.

| pet | feed |
|---|---|

1. ____________________

2. ____________________

**Write** the correct verb from the box in each sentence.

| walk | eats |
|---|---|

3. My dog ____________________ food.

4. We ____________________ in the park.

**Notes for Home:** Your child used verbs—words that name actions—in sentences. ***Home Activity:*** Look at photographs or pictures from magazines with your child. Have him or her use verbs in sentences that describe the pictures.

Name ______________________



RETEACHING

Add **-s** to the verb.

The girl **waters** the plant.

The boy **hits** the ball.

A **verb** may tell what one person, animal, or thing does.

**Read** the sentence.
**Write** the word on the line.

build builds

1. One pig ______________ a house.

blow blows

2. A wolf ______________ the house down.

make makes

3. One pig ______________ a house of sticks.

comes come

4. This house ______________ down too.

**Notes for Home:** Your child identified and wrote verbs to show the action of one animal or thing. ***Home Activity:*** Talk with your child about what you did today. Have him or her identify the verbs in your sentences.

Name ______________________________

**Draw** a line to the correct verb.

| | |
|---|---|
| 1. The teacher ______ at the girls. | **smiles**<br>**smile** |
| 2. The teacher ______ the children. | **help**<br>**helps** |
| 3. She ______ a book. | **read**<br>**reads** |
| 4. The teacher ______ to the children. | **talks**<br>**talk** |
| 5. The boy ______ on a chair. | **sit**<br>**sits** |



**Notes for Home:** Your child chose the correct verbs for sentences. ***Home Activity:*** Say sentences with singular subjects. (For example: *The cat jumps.*) Have your child repeat the verb in each sentence. *(jumps)*

Name ______________________________



RETEACHING

The people **work**.

Two foxes **run**.

Do not add **-s** to a verb that tells what two or more people, animals, or things do.

**Read** the first sentence.
**Write** the verb in the second sentence.

1. He plants one flower.

   They ________________ many flowers.

2. He waters his flower.

   They ________________ their flowers.

3. His flower grows tall.

   Their flowers ________________ tall.

**Notes for Home:** Your child identified verbs in sentences with plural subjects. ***Home Activity:*** Write plural subjects on cards. *(The dogs, The pigs)* Have your child write a sentence for each subject.

Name ______________________

**Circle** the correct word for each sentence.
**Write** the sentence.

1. The children __________. looks look

2. The winds __________. blow blows

3. Many leaves __________. falls fall

4. Some girls __________ the leaves. rake rakes

5. Those boys __________ the basket. hold holds

6. The puppies __________ in the pile! jumps jump

**Notes for Home:** Your child identified verbs that show the action of two or more people, animals, or things. ***Home Activity:*** Look at photographs of groups of people. Have your child say a sentence that describes what the people are doing in each photograph.

Name ______________________________

**RETEACHING**

She **claps.** (now) She **clapped.** (past)

Verbs can tell about action that takes place now.
Verbs can tell about action that happened in the past.

**Look** at each word in the boxes.
Does it tell about now or the past?
**Write** it under **Now** or **The Past**.

| Now | The Past |
|---|---|
| 1. | 2. |
| 3. | 4. |
| 5. | 6. |

| barked | calls | walked |
|---|---|---|
| jumps | needs | shouted |

**Notes for Home:** Your child identified verbs in the past and present tenses. ***Home Activity:*** Read a story with your child. Have him or her point out past-tense and present-tense verbs in the story.

Name ______________________________

**Circle** the correct word in ( ).

**1.** Last year he never (talks/talked).

**2.** Now he (talked/talks) too much.

**3.** Last year he never (walked/walks).

**4.** Now he (walked/walks) too much.

**5.** Last year he never (waves/waved).

**6.** Now he (waved/waves) too much.

**7.** Last year he never (jumps/jumped).

**8.** Now he (jumps/jumped) on me!

**Notes for Home:** Your child chose verbs in the past and present tenses to complete sentences. ***Home Activity:*** Sing a favorite song with your child. Have him or her identify past-tense and present-tense verbs in the song.

Name ______________________________

RETEACHING

A box **is** big.
Some toys **are** small.
The day **was** fun.
We **were** happy.

The words **is** and **are** tell about now.
Use **is** to tell about **one.**
Use **are** to tell about **more than one.**
The words **was** and **were** tell about the past.
Use **was** to tell about **one.**
Use **were** to tell about **more than one.**

**Draw** a line to complete each sentence.

| | |
|---|---|
| **1.** The party | were pretty. |
| **2.** The birthday signs | is over. |
| **3.** Carlos | is happy. |
| **4.** The games | is gone! |
| **5.** The cake | are put away. |

**Notes for Home:** Your child used correct forms of the verb *to be* in sentences. ***Home Activity:*** Together, make up a poem about family members. Have your child tell you which forms of the verb *to be* to use.

Name ____________________

**Use** the words in the boxes to complete the sentences.
One word will be used twice.

1. The dogs ______________ outside.

2. The birds ______________ on the grass.

3. The tree ______________ empty.

4. Now one bird ______________ outside.

5. The kittens ______________ small.

| was | are | is | were |
|---|---|---|---|

**Notes for Home:** Your child used correct forms of the verb *to be*, such as *is, are, was,* and *were,* in sentences. ***Home Activity:*** Together, read a favorite story. Ask your child to point out where different forms of the verb *to be* are used in the story.

Name ______________________________

**RETEACHING**

A verb and the word **not** can be put together to make a contraction.
An **'** is used in place of the letter *o*.

is not = **isn't**     are not = **aren't**

A **contraction** is a short way to put two words together.

**Read** each sentence.
**Write** the contraction for the underlined words.

1. The sun did not come out. ______________

2. Our pond was not full. ______________

3. It is not warm. ______________

4. The boys are not glad. ______________

5. My dogs are not sleeping. ______________

6. The day is not fun. ______________

**Notes for Home:** Your child wrote contractions using *not* with verbs. ***Home Activity:*** Say a sentence, using the verb *is, are, was, were, do,* or *did. (I was at the store.)* Have your child change the sentence by using a contraction of the verb and the word *not. (I wasn't at the store.)*

Name ______________________________

## Word Bank

is not = isn't  are not = aren't

was not = wasn't  were not = weren't

**Read** each sentence.
**Write** the two words for each contraction.

1. The farm wasn't noisy.

2. Birds aren't flying.

3. The sky isn't dark.

4. The cows aren't mooing.

5. Our chicken isn't clucking.

6. Fields weren't plowed.

7. Aunt Marge wasn't coming.

**Write** a sentence. Use a contraction.

**Notes for Home:** Your child separated contractions of verbs and the word *not*. *(isn't, aren't, wasn't, weren't)* ***Home Activity:*** Sing a familiar song with your child. Change the words by using contractions of verbs and the word *not*.

Name ______________________________

RETEACHING

**hot** fire

An **adjective** tells more about a person, place, or thing.

**Circle** the adjective that tells about each picture.

1. **big** cat **small** cat
2. **sad** girl **happy** girl

3. **slow** rocket **fast** rocket
4. **funny** clown **sleepy** clown

5. **big** animal **tiny** animal
6. happy man **wet** man

**Notes for Home:** Your child identified adjectives—words that describe. ***Home Activity:*** Point to objects in the room. Have your child use adjectives to describe the objects.

Name ______________________

**Read** each sentence.
**Choose** an adjective from the box to complete each sentence.
**Write** the word on the line.

| big | black | long | little |
|---|---|---|---|

1. The boys ride a ____________ bike.

2. They see a ____________ bus.

3. The ____________ dog walks with the girl.

4. The dog wears a ____________ bow.

**Notes for Home:** Your child used adjectives in sentences. ***Home Activity:*** Have your child draw an imaginary creature. Then ask him or her to use adjectives to label the drawing.

Name ______________________

The water is **blue**. The **yellow** sun is hot.

Some adjectives describe colors.

The ball is **round**.

Some adjectives describe shapes.

**Draw** a line under each color word.
**Color** each picture.

1. The red truck goes fast.

2. The yellow sun is big.

3. The green leaves cover the tree.

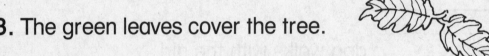

**Circle** each word that describes a shape.

4. The square box was full.

5. The round Earth is pretty.

**Notes for Home:** Your child identified adjectives that describe colors and shapes. ***Home Activity:*** Have your child cut out pictures from magazines or catalogs. Then have him or her label the pictures with words that describe colors and shapes.

Name ______________________________

**Write** the color of each picture in the boxes.
**Write** one letter in each box.

| blue | green | orange | red | yellow |
|---|---|---|---|---|

1. 2. 3. 4. 5.

6. Write the new color word you made. ______________

| round | square |
|---|---|

7. **Write** a sentence, using a word that tells about a shape.

______________________________

______________________________

**Notes for Home:** Your child wrote adjectives that describe color and shape. ***Home Activity:*** Have your child write color and shape words on cards. Then have him or her place the cards near objects they describe.

Name ______________________

**RETEACHING**

big

small

Some **adjectives** describe size.
The words **big, small, long, short,** and **tiny** describe size.

**Write** an adjective for each picture.

1. 

______________________

2. 

______________________

3. 

______________________

4. 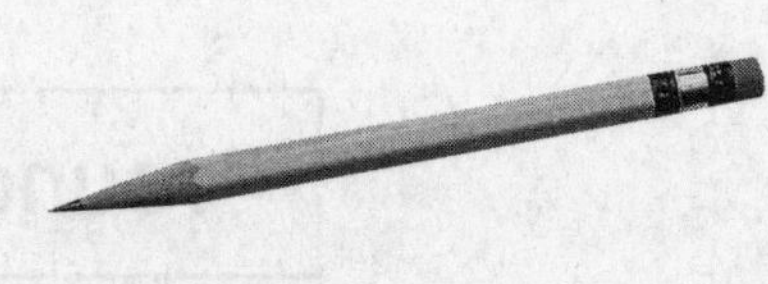

______________________

**Notes for Home:** Your child wrote adjectives that describe size. ***Home Activity:*** Have two friends or family members stand next to each other. Then have your child tell about them, using adjectives that describe size.

Name ______________________________

| small | big | tiny | short | tall |
|---|---|---|---|---|

**Look** at the pictures. Write an adjective for each sentence.

1. The dog has a ______________ tail.

2. The ______________ cat looks at the dog.

3. The ______________ dog looks at the cat.

4. A boy paints a ______________ fence.

**Notes for Home:** Your child wrote adjectives that describe size. ***Home Activity:*** Have your child look in a story for adjectives that describe size. Then have him or her make up sentences, using the adjectives from the story.

Name ______________________________

**RETEACHING**

This mop is **wet**.

The **happy** pup jumps.

An **adjective** can tell what kind.

**Read** each sentence.
**Circle** the adjective or adjectives.

1. The hat is old.

2. Nan gets a new hat.

3. The new hat is pretty.

4. It has funny flowers on top.

5. Now Nan is happy!

**Notes for Home:** Your child identified adjectives that tell what kind. ***Home Activity:*** Together, make up a story about an imaginary place. Have your child use adjectives to describe what kinds of things someone visiting the place might see.

Name ______________________________

**Read** each sentence.
**Choose** the correct adjective in ( ).
**Write** it on the line.

1. I like to pet the (soft/hard) rabbit.

2. The children are (sad/happy).

3. The (fast/slow) snail is moving.

4. This duck was very (bad/good)!

5. Don't touch the (hot/cold) fire!

6. That is a (long/sad) bat.

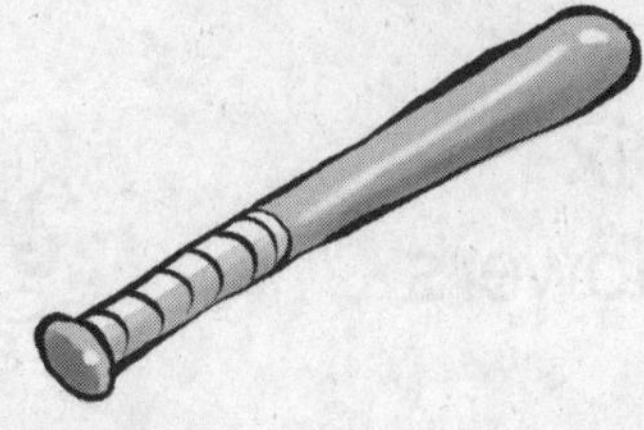

**Notes for Home:** Your child identified appropriate adjectives—words that describe—in sentences. ***Home Activity:*** Put three objects on a table. (For example: apple, orange, banana) Have your child use adjectives in sentences to describe what kinds of objects they are.

Name ______________________________

**three** balls

Some **adjectives** tell how many.

**Draw** a line from the adjective to the picture.

1. **five** bees 
2. **one** sun 
3. **three** birds 
4. **ten** trees 
5. **six** flowers 
6. **two** houses 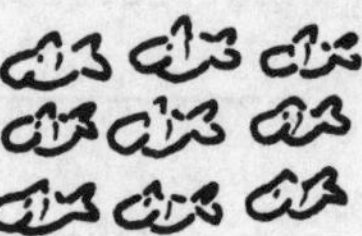
7. **seven** dolls 
8. **nine** fish 
9. **four** bicycles 
10. **eight** wagons 

**Notes for Home:** Your child identified adjectives that tell how many. ***Home Activity:*** Have your child draw a picture of groups of things. Then have him or her count items in the drawing and label the drawing with number words.

Name ______________________

**Answer** each question.
**Write** the number word.

1. How many cats are by the door?

______________________

2. How many frogs jump?

______________________

3. How many birds are in the tree?

______________________

4. How many dogs have nothing to do?

______________________

**Notes for Home:** Your child wrote adjectives that tell how many. ***Home Activity:*** Write two questions for your child that will require numbers as answers. *(How many clocks are in our home?)* Have your child write each answer in a complete sentence.

Name ______________________

**RETEACHING**

The **fat** pig eats food.

An **adjective** tells more about a person, place, or thing.

**Read** each sentence.
**Write** the adjective in each sentence.

1. A tall giraffe wears a tie.

2. A big baboon eats a pie.

3. A lion scares a tiny flea.

4. A wet hippo drinks tea.



**Notes for Home:** Your child wrote adjectives—words that describe. ***Home Activity:*** Ask your child to use adjectives to describe things he or she saw at school today.

Name ______________________________

**Finish** the caption for each picture.
**Write** the best adjective to complete each sentence.

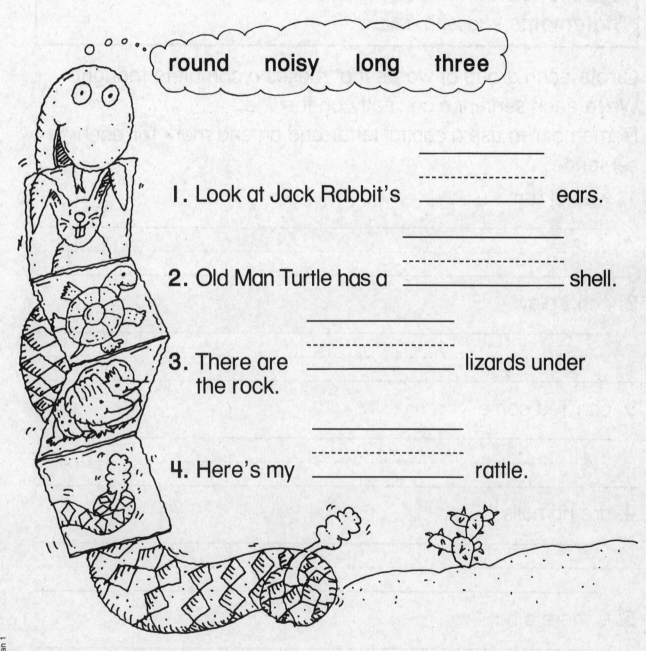

round noisy long three

1. Look at Jack Rabbit's ______________ ears.

2. Old Man Turtle has a ______________ shell.

3. There are ______________ lizards under the rock.

4. Here's my ______________ rattle.

**Notes for Home:** Your child wrote adjectives in sentences. ***Home Activity:*** Have your child draw himself or herself. Then have him or her use adjectives to write a description of the drawing.

Name ______________________

**RETEACHING**

A **sentence** tells a complete idea.
It begins with a **capital letter.**
**Questions** end with a **?**.
**Statements** end with a **.**.

**Circle** each group of words that makes a complete thought.
**Write** each sentence correctly on the line.
Remember to use a capital letter and an end mark for each sentence.

1. we will run

______________________

2. can I play

______________________

3. can Ted come

______________________

4. are no balls

______________________

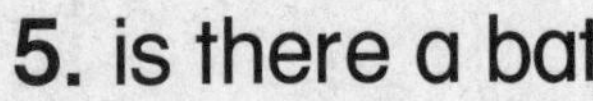

5. is there a bat

______________________

**Notes for Home:** Your child correctly wrote statements and questions. ***Home Activity:*** Have your child explain rules for writing statements and questions correctly.

Name ______________________________

**Read** each group of words.
**Circle** each group of words that makes a complete sentence.

1. Are apples.
2. Lunch is good.
3. Can I eat too?
4. Is hungry.
5. Did Dad make it?
6. I helped cook lunch.

**Change** each telling sentence into an asking sentence.

It is four o'clock. Is it four o'clock?

7. There are apples.

______________________________

8. This is for me.

______________________________

**Notes for Home:** Your child correctly identified complete sentences. ***Home Activity:*** Say three questions to your child. Have him or her write them. Then help your child turn each question into a statement.

Name ______________________________

**RETEACHING**

An **exclamation** is a sentence that shows strong feeling.
It begins with a capital letter.
It ends with **!**.

**I'm so scared!**

**Read** each sentence.
**Write** the exclamation on the line.

1. I need some help. Help me!

______________________________

2. I'm having a great time! This is fun.

______________________________

3. Leave me alone! Please leave.

______________________________

4. I feel good. I'm so happy!

______________________________

5. Look out! You should be careful.

______________________________

**Notes for Home:** Your child identified and wrote exclamations—sentences that show strong feeling. ***Home Activity:*** Ask your child to write short sentences that show strong, happy feelings and that end with exclamation marks (*!*).

Name ______________________________



**Look** at each picture.
**Write** an exclamation about it.

1.

2.

3.

4.

5.

**Notes for Home:** Your child wrote exclamations—sentences that express strong feeling. ***Home Activity:*** Write an exclamation and have your child act it out. Then change roles.

Name ______________________________

RETEACHING

Go to bed.

One kind of sentence is called a **command**.
A **command** tells someone to do something.
It ends with a **.**.

**Draw** a picture for each command.

1. Eat your dinner.
2. Please come here.
3. Get in line.
4. Please read this book to me.

**Write** a command.
**Draw** a picture of it.

5. ______________________________

**Notes for Home:** Your child showed understanding of commands by illustrating them. ***Home Activity:*** Have your child write commands that lead to a treasure. *(Take ten steps. Open the cupboard. Look on the shelf. Find the cookie.)*

Name ______________________________

**Draw** a line under each command.

1. Please come here.
2. Are you happy today?
3. When are we going?
4. Help me with this.
5. You are my friend.
6. Put on your coat.
7. Turn off the light.
8. What time is it?
9. Tell me what time it is.

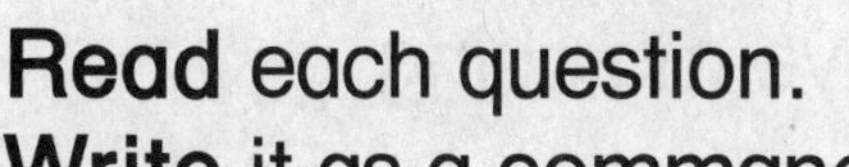

**Read** each question.
**Write** it as a command.

10. Will you play ball?

______________________________

11. Can you help Mark?

______________________________

12. Will you go there?

______________________________

**Notes for Home:** Your child identified and wrote commands. ***Home Activity:*** Have your child make up an imaginary pet. Then help him or her write commands for the pet. *(Come here. Eat your carrots.)*

Name ______________________________



**RETEACHING**

**The mother** cooks breakfast.
**She** cooks breakfast.

**The boy** eats an apple.
**He** eats an apple.

**The glass** holds water.
**It** holds water.

**He, she, it, I, we, you,** and **they** can take the place of nouns. They are called **pronouns.**

**Draw** a line to connect sentences that have matching meanings.

| | |
|---|---|
| 1. The boys read a book. | He hears the story. |
| 2. The book is very big. | They read a book. |
| 3. A man hears the story. | It is very big. |
| 4. My sister and I clean. | We clean. |
| 5. A car comes. | She says hello. |
| 6. The girl says hello. | It comes. |

**Notes for Home:** Your child identified sentences with pronouns. ***Home Activity:*** Read a sentence from a story to your child. *(The rabbit hopped away.)* Have him or her replace a noun in the sentence with a pronoun, and say the new sentence. *(It hopped away.)*

Name ______________________________

**Circle** the correct word in each box.
**Write** it in each sentence.

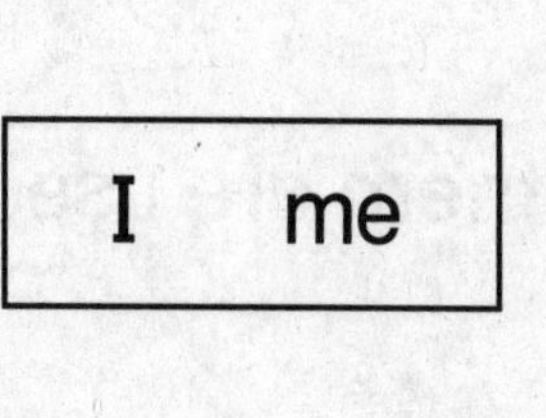

I me

1. Sally sees Mrs. Bear and __________.

We it

2. __________ say hello to Sally.

It They

3. ______ is big and dark.

**Notes for Home:** Your child wrote pronouns in sentences. ***Home Activity:*** Have your child write a short poem about two animals or people. Challenge him or her to use pronouns in the poem.

Name ______________________

**RETEACHING**

A **pronoun** can take the place of some words in a sentence.
**I, he, she, we,** and **they** are used in the **naming part** of a sentence.
**Me, him, her, us,** and **them** are used in the action part of the sentence.

**We** take **them**.

**Read** each sentence.
**Choose** a pronoun to replace each underlined group of words.
**Write** the pronoun on the line.

1. Sarah and I are going to begin a play. ____________

2. The play is about my brother. ____________

3. My brother is funny. ____________

4. My parents are going to watch. ____________

5. The play is for my parents. ____________

**Notes for Home:** Your child wrote personal pronouns correctly. ***Home Activity:*** Look at pictures of people from magazines with your child. Have your child describe the pictures, using personal pronouns in sentences.

Name ______________________

**Read** each sentence.
**Circle** the correct word in ( ).
**Write** it on the line.

---

1. (I/me) got a snake today. __________

2. A man told (I/me) about the snake. __________

3. (We/It) looked at the snake. __________

4. The snake looked at (her/us). __________

5. I gave water to (it/me). __________

**Notes for Home:** Your child wrote personal pronouns that fit in sentences. ***Home Activity:*** Together, find personal pronouns in a favorite story. Then have your child make up new sentences, using the personal pronouns from the story.

Name ______________________

**RETEACHING**

one bow

two bows

An **-s** makes a noun mean more than one.

Pretend that you need to buy more than one of each item listed. **Write** the correct noun.

## Shopping List

candle

1. ______________________

cupcake

2. ______________________

egg

3. ______________________

present

4. ______________________

card

5. ______________________

**Notes for Home:** Your child wrote plural forms of nouns. ***Home Activity:*** Have your child make a list of things two people might need if they were to go on a trip to a cold place. Remind your child to use plural forms of nouns.

Name ______________________________

**Look** for each musical instrument.
**Write** the number and naming word to complete each sentence.

drum drums

1. I spy ______________________.

bell bells

2. I spy ______________________.

guitars guitar

3. I spy ______________________.

shaker shakers

4. I spy ______________________.

**Notes for Home:** Your child wrote plural forms of nouns in sentences. ***Home Activity:*** Together, write a story about plants and animals. Challenge your child to use plural nouns in two sentences.